SKYWARD BOUND

Matt Ralphs

Illustrated by **Matt Rockefeller**

OXFORD
UNIVERSITY PRESS

As a writer I'm often asked where I get my ideas from. My answer is: Everywhere and Nowhere.

Nowhere is my imagination; that cave deep inside my brain where ideas drip from the roof to form crooked stalagmites in the darkness. These stalagmites sometimes, *sometimes*, coagulate into story ideas.

But where do the ideas that form the stalagmites come from? Well, they come from Everywhere: films, TV, comics, music, history, and people – friends, family, and strangers seen from afar.

It was a member of my family who inspired *Skyward Bound* and the character of Gerald. Just like Gerald, Neville was a little eccentric and cut a dash wherever he went.

This book is for him.

Matt Ralphs

Chapter One

The beeping alarm wrenched Jake Osborne from a vivid dream about flying a Spitfire.

He lay half-awake in bed, remembering the cramped cockpit, the smell of oil, the wind whistling over the canopy and the engine's roar in his ears ...

Shaking off his sleepiness, Jake reached out and turned the alarm off. Grey daylight filtered through the rain-splattered window.

'Monday morning, oh *great*,' he groaned.

He gazed up at the model planes suspended on thread from the ceiling: a Spitfire, a Hurricane and a Lancaster bomber. Jake had built them himself, even painting the little pilots before sealing them in with glue. For a moment, he imagined taking off in his own plane and flying far, far away.

The sound of voices and breakfast being prepared drifted up from downstairs. Mum and Steve were already awake. Jake dragged himself out of bed and started to put on his school uniform. The floorboards were cold against his feet so he hurried to put on his socks.

Steve's house still felt strange. Jake and his mum had only moved in a few weeks ago and there were a few boxes left to unpack. It was more of a cottage, with creaking floors and central heating that failed to warm the bedrooms. Even the view was weird. Instead of houses and shops, it was all fields, hedges and trees.

New town, new house … new school.

Jake sighed, knotted his school tie, and went downstairs.

Jake's mum was at the kitchen table warming her hands around a mug of tea. 'Morning, love,' she said. 'All ready for school?' She was smiling but Jake saw the worry in her eyes.

'Sure, Mum,' he said in his brightest voice. 'Can't wait!'

Steve turned from the sink. 'Morning, squadron leader!' he said, giving a salute. 'Ready for take-off?'

Jake cringed and forced himself to return the salute. 'Morning, Steve.'

Jake had decided Steve was OK when Mum started going out with him three years ago. He had a good job (something to do with IT), sometimes took Jake to the cinema and had even built him a fantastic gaming computer. But most importantly for Jake, Steve made Mum happy again.

But ever since they'd moved into his house Steve had started to try too hard. He was so eager for Jake to relax and settle in that it was having the opposite effect. And this new saluting thing? It *had* to stop before Jake died of embarrassment.

'Don't forget, it's my sister's birthday bash tonight,' Steve said. 'There's someone going who I want you to meet.'

'Oh? Who?' Jake raised his eyebrows.

Steve tapped the side of his nose. 'It's a surprise,' he said, turning back to the washing up.

'Got anything good on at school today?' Mum said, the worry still stirring behind her eyes.

'Sure,' Jake said, putting on his best smile. 'English, Maths. You know, the usual.'

'And you're making friends?'

'Loads,' Jake said as he poured himself some cereal. 'I'm trying out for the football team on Wednesday.'

'Great,' Steve said over his shoulder. 'We'll come and watch you play.'

Mum's eyes didn't leave Jake's face. 'I know it's hard starting a new school halfway through the year, being the new boy, trying to fit in … '

'Mum, I'm fine. Really.'

'But if you weren't, you'd tell me, wouldn't you?'

'Of course.' Desperate to end this gentlest of interrogations, Jake finished the last spoonful of cereal, got up and grabbed his coat and school bag from the back of the chair. 'Now stop worrying.'

'Mothers always worry about their sons,' Steve said. 'It's an unchanging rule of the universe.'

'Right. I'd better go or I'll be late. Bye!' Jake escaped out of the back door with Steve calling after him, 'Don't forget the party tonight! You can bring a friend if you like.'

It was a cold, windy day, with the fields on either side of the road barely visible behind grey drizzle. *Bad flying weather*, Jake thought, putting up his hood and heading towards town. He walked on past the farm, the little post office and the war memorial.

He was already late for school, but as usual his pace slackened the closer he got. His shoulders slumped. His feet dragged. Dread settled like a boulder in his stomach as he turned the final corner.

It loomed at the end of the road: a flat-roofed building and playground surrounded by a high wire fence. To Jake it looked more like a prison than a school. Children stood in groups, chatting, laughing and waiting for the bell to ring. A few were playing football, which reminded Jake of the lie he'd told about joining the school team.

The rain got harder as he sloped through the gates. No one called his name or waved as he made his way to the corner of the playground, where he sat alone on a low brick wall.

No one even noticed him.

Chapter Two

'Well, here we are.' Steve turned the car into a wide stone gateway. 'It's party time.'

Hawthorne House, where Steve's sister lived, stood at the end of a long gravel drive surrounded by what looked like acres of parkland and trees.

'Wow,' Jake said. 'This is some house!'

'It certainly is. My sister runs a successful business with her husband. She is passionate about helping people so they spend a lot of time organizing events and parties to raise money for charities. She's brilliant at it.'

Mum, wearing her best dress and with her hair specially straightened, turned from the front seat. 'They're both really nice and they're looking forward to meeting you, Jake.' She smiled. 'And you look *so* handsome in your suit and lovely tie.'

Jake thought it bad enough that he had to wear school uniform all day without being forced into a blue suit the moment he'd got home. Not only that, the 'lovely tie' was yellow and the brown spot pattern made it look as if he'd spilled a cup of tea down it.

As they drew close to the house, Jake's eyes were drawn to the gleaming ranks of parked cars, powerful, sleek and shiny. 'I knew I should have given mine a clean,' Steve muttered as he pulled into a space under an oak tree.

The day's rain had cleared and Jake stepped out into a bright but chilly evening. Mum handed him a bunch of flowers. 'Give these to Carol when you're introduced. It'll be a nice way for you to break the ice.'

'Mum, who is it that Steve wants me to meet? Tell me – you know I don't like surprises.'

But Mum only grinned. 'You'll see!'

The grand front door opened before they even reached the bottom step and a woman who looked uncannily like Steve sashayed down the steps. *'Hello!'* she cooed, wrapping her arms around Steve and kissing his cheek. 'How lovely to see you all. Oh, Sophie, what a *gorgeous* dress.'

'Thanks, Carol. I'd like you to meet my son, Jake.'

'Jake! How marvellous to meet you at last,' Carol beamed. 'Welcome to Hawthorne House! *Love* the tie – very chic.'

'Hello, Mrs Travers,' Jake said, dutifully holding out the flowers and feeling a bit better about his tie. 'Thank you for inviting me to your party.'

'Oh, it's more of a soirée really – very low key,' Carol said with a modest shrug. 'And we'll have none of this Mrs Travers business if you don't mind. Jake, you simply *must* call me Carol.'

'OK, I will do, er, Carol,' Jake replied, wondering what a 'soirée' was.

They followed Carol into a huge lobby with marble floors, wood-panelled walls and a wide central staircase leading to the first floor landing. Lots of people stood chatting in little groups, eating nibbles from plates passed round by a team of smartly uniformed caterers.

Jake sighed. No kids, just adults. It looked like he wouldn't be making any friends this evening. *Just like at school*, he thought.

'Hey, Carol,' Steve said. 'Is the special guest here?'

'He *is*,' Carol whispered.

'So I think it's time we introduced him to Jake, don't you?' nudged Steve.

'Oh yes, we absolutely *must*!' Carol said. 'He's outside, I think.'

'Who is?' Jake said.

'Our grandad,' Carol replied. 'We've not seen him for absolutely years.'

'Not since we were teenagers,' Steve added.

'He's been living in Germany but he's moved back to Kent. We're absolutely *thrilled* because he was always such a sweetheart and he's really not changed a bit.'

Jake tried to look interested despite not understanding why they were so keen to introduce him to their ancient, long-lost relative.

'The thing is,' Mum said, 'he was in the RAF during World War Two.'

'O-oh,' Jake said, beginning to understand. 'Was he a pilot?'

'We think so,' Steve said, 'but we've never really talked to him about it.'

'We were hoping, as someone who loves planes, you'd be able to find out for us,' Carol said. 'I bet he's got some fascinating tales to tell. So, would you like to meet a fighter pilot, or some of my husband's friends?'

Jake smiled. 'I'll take the pilot.'

'Fab!' Carol said. 'Come with me then, Jake.'

Leaving Mum and Steve to mingle, Jake followed Carol through some French doors and out on to the perfectly maintained back garden, complete with a stunning view of the rolling South Downs.

'Ah, there he is.' Carol pointed towards a summerhouse where a silver-haired man was sitting on a wicker chair, gazing up at the sky. 'Grandad! I've someone here I'd like you to meet.'

Feeling a bit awkward, Jake followed in her wake.

Chapter Three

'Gerald, meet Jake,' Carol beamed. 'Jake, meet Gerald, our lost sheep returned to the fold.'

Gerald, dapperly dressed in a suit, red waistcoat and gleaming shoes, smiled and sprang up from the chair. 'Pleased to meet you, Jake.' He held out his hand, but then swiftly withdrew it. 'You've not been sent to keep an eye on me, have you?'

'No,' Jake said, a bit nonplussed. 'Not that I know of, anyway.'

'Thank heavens for that.' Gerald's eyes glinted as he held out his hand again. 'I don't like any fuss, as I keep telling Carol and Steve. That's why I'm hiding in the summerhouse!'

'Oh, Gerald,' Carol said, 'we're not *that* bad.'

'I know you're not, Carol. But some of your friends are a bit boring, so I'll stay put for now, if you don't mind.'

'You're terrible!' Carol gave him a kiss on the cheek. She turned to Jake. 'Would you believe this old rogue is in his *nineties*?'

Jake couldn't. With his bright eyes and straight back, Gerald looked twenty years younger.

'I wonder what his secret is,' Carol continued. 'And if

it's some sort of miracle anti-ageing cream, then why is he withholding it from me?'

Gerald waved his hand at her. 'I've told you my secret – long walks, always seeing the bright side of things and a big bowl of prunes for breakfast.'

'Yuck,' Carol said. 'Now then, Gerald, Jake here absolutely *adores* planes and he's dying to know all about your time in the RAF. So I'll leave you to it while I go back to my boring friends.' She winked then headed back to the house.

'We may have just met, Jake,' Gerald said, settling back into his chair, 'but I know something about you already. That dreadful tie you're wearing – you didn't choose it yourself. Am I right?'

Jake sat on the chair next to him. 'It was my mum's choice.' He glanced at Gerald's tie, which had diagonal blue and maroon stripes with little gold eagles all over it. RAF colours.

'So, you're interested in planes, are you?' Gerald said.

'Absolutely,' Jake replied. 'I love jet planes, especially the American ones like the F14 Tomcat. But I love prop planes the best. My favourite's the Spitfire. Steve took me to Duxford airfield last summer and I saw *seventeen* of them fly over all at once. The sound they made was ... ' He tailed off. 'Indescribable.'

Gerald looked at Jake with a faint look of surprise. 'That's the engine for you. To me a Spit always sounded like a big cat. A lion or a tiger. From a distance they purr, but when they fly overhead ... they *roar*.'

'That's exactly right,' Jake said, his eyes shining. 'I felt that roar right here, in my chest.'

'Beautiful planes,' Gerald said wistfully, as he seemed to drift off.

Jake thought of the photographs he'd studied of World War Two fighter pilots, posing by their aircraft, or lounging in deckchairs by the runway waiting for the next alert. He'd been struck by how young they looked and had learned that their average age was only twenty.

Jake looked at Gerald's swept-back hair and neat moustache. He could almost imagine him seventy years ago in flying kit, helmet and goggles.

'Everyone's saying you were in the RAF during the war,' he said.

Gerald refocused his bright eyes back on to Jake. 'I was just eighteen when I enlisted in 1939, as soon as the balloon went up.' Jake looked blank. Gerald smiled. 'When the war started, I mean.'

'So you were actually *in* the Battle of Britain?' Jake asked, leaning eagerly forward.

'Oh yes. I was proud to serve my country.'

'It must be amazing to look back and realize you're part of history.' Jake shook his head in wonderment. 'One of the Few.'

Gerald raised his eyebrows. 'The Few?'

'Yes, you know, the Few. That's what Winston Churchill called the pilots who fought in the Battle of Britain. "Never in the field of human conflict was so much ... "'

'" ... owed by so many to so few,"' Gerald finished. 'Yes, I know the quote.'

Jake beamed. 'And that's you! One of the Few.'

A smile spread across Gerald's good-natured face. 'Well, if you say so.'

Before Jake could ask the first of the many questions queuing up in his head, one of the caterers brought over a dish of party nibbles.

After filling his plate, Gerald said, 'It's nice to meet someone so interested in history. I'm going to the Battle of Britain museum at Hawkinge this weekend. Why don't you and Steve come along too?'

'Oh yes, I'd like that!' Jake said. 'I've never been. I'll go and ask him right now!'

Chapter Four

It was all arranged. Gerald was to pick Steve and Jake up on Saturday morning for a trip to Hawkinge, but only if Jake had done his homework beforehand.

So on Friday evening Jake sat at the dining-room table, trying to finish his Science assignment. His new school was teaching more advanced science than his old one and he was finding it hard to catch up with his classmates.

He was about to throw the textbook across the room in hopeless frustration when Mum came in, still wearing her nurse's uniform, and plonked a mug of hot chocolate down for him. Her shoulders were slumped and her eyes were a little red, so Jake knew it had been a tiring shift at the hospital.

'How's it going?' she asked.

'Nearly finished,' he replied, carefully closing his workbook to hide his messy work and crossings out. 'It's all pretty easy actually.'

'That's good, because if you want to be a pilot you need to know your science.' She patted his hand. 'So anyway, I've been so busy with my shifts I forgot to ask: how did the football trials go?'

'Oh yeah, right,' Jake said, his insides squirming. 'Really well, I think. I scored a goal and Mr Hodges says my speed will be useful. But they don't announce the team until next week, so ... '

'Well, that's great. I'm so proud of you for adjusting to all this change. I know it's not been easy.'

A tide of worry surged up through Jake's chest, swelling his throat and making it hard to swallow. He felt an urge to spill it all out: how he missed his old friends; how much he hated his new school where no one ever spoke to him; how far behind he was with his studies.

But then he remembered what it had been like after Dad died – the grief, the crying, the sleepless nights. Most of all he remembered the way Mum had seemed to shrink, as if all the joy inside had leaked away with her tears. Jake could hardly bear the memory. Then she'd met Steve and begun to grow again – and now that they were properly living together, Jake saw how happy she was.

There was no way he was going to spoil that by burdening her with his problems. *I've got to deal with them on my own,* he thought. So he swallowed all his worry down deep inside and lied again. 'It's all good, Mum. I'm doing great.'

'Good. So, Gerald's coming to pick you and Steve up tomorrow at about ten. He recently reapplied for his driving licence and apparently his friends in the village are most relieved because he's basically their free taxi service. He takes them to the shops and the doctors.'

'Oh, that's nice of him,' Jake said.

'It really is. So I've packed you all a nice lunch and you can do a flask of tea in the morning.' Her face grew serious. 'Now listen, Gerald's amazingly sprightly for someone in his nineties, but I want you to keep an eye on him. Make sure he doesn't overdo it. Will you do that for me?'

'Sure, Mum. And thanks for the drink.'

She smiled. 'All good boys deserve hot chocolate.'

Chapter Five

Gerald arrived with what Steve called 'military precision' at ten o'clock the next morning. The sun was out and already burning off the dew from the garden – a perfect day for an excursion.

'Come on, squadron leader,' Steve said. 'Our carriage awaits!'

Jake grabbed the lunches and flask, said goodbye to Mum and jogged down the drive to where Gerald waited in his car.

He was surprised to see it was a green sports car with the roof down. The engine throbbed under a long bonnet. Gerald, again smartly dressed but this time wearing a flat cap, reached over and opened the door.

'Morning,' he said. 'Hop in.'

Steve peered at the tiny back seat. 'Will Jake fit in there?'

'He won't need to,' Gerald said breezily. 'That's *your* seat. Jake's my co-pilot, so he sits in the front with me. Go on, Steve, in you squeeze.'

Gerald and Jake waited as Steve manoeuvred himself awkwardly into the back seat and settled with his knees jutting up just under his chin.

'Is it a long journey?' Steve asked dryly.

'This,' Jake said, 'is a nice car.'

'It certainly is,' Gerald replied. 'All strapped in? Good! Then off we go.'

Jake's back pressed into the seat as Gerald threw the car into gear and brought the engine to life. The Kentish countryside whirled past, sparkling in the morning sun.

'I fine-tuned the car myself,' Gerald said. 'Runs like a dream, doesn't it?'

'It's fantastic!' Jake raised his voice over the roar. 'I'm never going to drive a boring car – I want one just like this when I'm older!'

'That's the spirit.' Gerald pointed to a packet of biscuits on the dashboard. 'Time for elevenses, I think.'

'But it's only just after ten o'clock.'

'Ten-ses then. Go on – open them up. I'm starving.'

The three of them had finished most of the packet by the time they reached the Battle of Britain museum at the former RAF airbase at Hawkinge. Jake's face tingled from the open-air drive when he got out of the car.

Steve fought his way out of the back and jogged on the spot to get his legs working again.

'Ready?' Jake asked.

'You know,' Steve said, 'we passed a little cricket ground about half a mile back, and it looked like they were setting up for a match. I might just pop back there instead and catch up with you later, if you don't mind.'

'Oh, all right,' Jake said, actually quite pleased to be going to the museum just with Gerald. 'I'll give you a call on your mobile when we're finished here.'

'Great,' Steve said, heading for the gate. 'Don't hurry on my account.'

Gerald shook his head. 'Why would anyone want to watch a game of cricket when there are planes to look at?'

'Who knows?' Jake shrugged.

Gerald insisted on paying for Jake's ticket, as long as he spent some pocket money in the gift shop. 'We must support this place,' he said. 'It's an important link to our history.'

Tickets bought, they emerged from the office on to a grassy area dominated by the old hangar, a curved green building that looked like an enormous, partially buried pipe. Jake imagined what it must have been like when it was still a working airbase, with mechanics repairing planes, pilots gathering for their daily briefings, vapour trails criss-crossing the sky overhead ...

Three fighter planes stood on the grass, their canopies glinting in the sun.

'Hurricanes,' Jake said. 'I've never seen one so close before. Did you fly them?'

Gerald's gaze was so fixed on the nearest aircraft that he didn't seem to hear Jake's question. 'The workhorse of the RAF.' He reached out and touched a wingtip. 'Shot down more planes than the Spitfires, you know.'

Jake did know and he added that Hurricanes were built from wood and fabric, which made them prone to catching fire. Gerald looked impressed. 'You're dead right. You *do* know your stuff.'

Jake felt a glow of pride. 'Were you here during the war?'

'No, I was stationed at Biggin Hill – a bigger airbase.'

An idea struck Jake as they entered the hangar. 'Hey,' he said, 'if you tell the lady at the visitor entrance that you were a pilot, she might give us a special tour or something.'

'Oh, dear me no,' Gerald said. 'I don't want any kind of fuss. Besides, we're experts. We're the ones who should be giving a tour!'

The hangar was packed with exhibits: searchlights, engines and even more planes, some of which looked like they were fresh from the factory.

Jake and Gerald wandered round together, trading facts and figures. This turned into something of a friendly competition as they tried to outdo each other with their knowledge of planes. Gerald won, but Jake didn't mind.

At the far end of the hangar stood an armoured car with angled steel plates, four wheels and a turret. Jake wandered off to look at some gas masks, but when he turned round Gerald had disappeared.

'Gerald?' he said. He did a quick circuit of the hangar, but there was no sign of him. He returned to the armoured car, with Mum's request that he keep an eye on Gerald ringing in his ears. Where on earth *was* he?

Jake was about to go outside to continue the search when he saw a face peering out at him from one of the armoured car's slit windows.

'Gerald? What are you doing?' he hissed.

'I'm having a nice sit down,' Gerald replied.

'But you shouldn't be in there!'

'Why not?'

'Because there's a *rope* around it.'

'Oh, don't worry about that,' Gerald said breezily. 'I just hopped over.'

'But you might, you know, damage something.'

Gerald's laugh echoed out through the gun slits. 'This was built to survive a war! How could I possibly damage it? Come on in, Jake. The door's round this side.'

Jake knew it was wrong, but Gerald's logic also made perfect sense ... and he *was* curious to see inside. Checking to ensure there was no one around, Jake hopped over the rope and scurried between the car and the wall. The door was already open so he quickly climbed in. Gerald was sitting in the driver's seat. He unscrewed the flask.

'Tea?'

Chapter Six

Mum had packed egg sandwiches, cheese and yogurts, which the pair ate in the cramped but weirdly cosy confines of the armoured car. There were crisps too, but Jake said they'd better not eat them because the rustling of the packets might give them away.

'Very tasty, very sweet,' Gerald said, carefully wiping his moustache with a napkin. 'Thank you. That was a very fine lunch.'

Jake chewed thoughtfully on his sandwich. He'd hoped that Gerald would volunteer stories of his wartime piloting exploits, but so far he'd not said anything about them. Steve had warned Jake not to push Gerald too hard, because people who had lived through wars were sometimes reluctant to talk about it.

Jake understood this, but he was burning with curiosity. Reading books, watching documentaries and pouring over photos was fine, but Gerald had actually been *there*. Besides, he'd also been told that talking about tough experiences was beneficial, so wouldn't he be doing Gerald a favour by asking him some questions?

'Gerald,' Jake said, unpeeling a yogurt lid, 'how many patrols did you fly when you were at Biggin Hill?'

'Oh, you don't want to hear about all that.' Gerald's eyes flicked to the door. 'Perhaps we'd better make a move ... '

'We can't yet. There's some people over there, so we'll have to wait. Oh go on, tell me. It'll be really useful for my schoolwork.'

'School, eh? I had a great time at school,' Gerald said. 'What's yours like? I bet it's great, isn't it?'

The mention of school brought all the loneliness Jake thought he'd locked away for the weekend flooding back. He swallowed hard, suddenly filled with panic that he was going to lose it in front of his new friend.

My only friend, he thought, as tears prickled behind his eyes. He tried to speak but the words seemed to get lodged in his throat.

'Oh dear.' Gerald's voice was gentle. 'Having a rough time, are you?'

Jake looked down at his hands and nodded.

'Do you want to talk about it, old chap?' Gerald said, handing him his handkerchief.

'Thanks,' Jake whispered and blew his nose. 'No, it's OK, I feel better now.'

'That's the ticket.'

Jake took a deep breath and managed a smile. 'Sorry, I didn't mean to ... '

'Nothing to be ashamed of. We all get down from time to time.' Gerald shifted in his seat. 'I'm getting a bit of a cramp. Why don't we go outside?'

Timing their escape so they didn't get seen, they left the armoured car and went to sit on a bench overlooking the Hurricanes. The sun was warm on Jake's face and he began to feel better.

'Would it cheer you up if I told you about something that happened during the war?' Gerald said.

'Definitely!' Jake said, brightening up even more.

'Well, this is something that happened in July 1940.'

'At the start of the Battle of Britain.'

'Indeed. It was a warm day, just like today, with not a cloud in the sky. It was actually hard to believe that we were at war. Anyway, the enemy were constantly bombing our ships from their captured French airbases, so we'd been sent on patrol over the English Channel to see what was happening.'

Jake was already enraptured. 'What were you flying?'

'Oh, a Spitfire. There were five of us. I was the youngest pilot in the squadron and this was one of my first patrols.'

'Were you scared?'

Gerald thought for a moment. 'Not once I was in the air. After that my training took over. I had a job to do and that was that.'

'I bet I'd be scared,' Jake said. 'Up there on my own.'

'Ah, but I wasn't on my own – I had my mates with me and I knew they'd be looking out for me.' Gerald gave Jake a good-natured jab in the ribs. 'Are you going to keep interrupting me, or let me carry on with the story?'

'Sorry.'

'All right then ... We were heading out over the sea when we saw six black specks in the sky, diving down on to us. Messerschmitt 109s! Fighters!'

Jake's eyes widened.

'Well, the sky was suddenly filled with planes, whirling and diving,' Gerald continued. 'We'd been taken completely by surprise. I went into a dive to pick up some speed and suddenly *BAM!* The plane bucked like a mule and I heard the sound of tearing metal.'

'You'd been hit?' Jake said breathlessly.

'I certainly had. I saw great holes in my wing, and then the engine started to hitch and smoke. Then, I don't mind telling you, I got pretty scared.'

'What happened next?'

'I was lucky. My wingman chased away the fighter who'd shot me. I turned my nose for home, but my plane was so badly wounded I knew I'd never make it. I was wearing my oxygen mask so I could breathe through the smoke, but even with my goggles on I couldn't see a thing!

And then, all of a sudden, I saw flickers of orange – the engine was on fire.'

Gerald paused for a moment, deep in thought. Jake waited for him to continue.

'I couldn't think straight. It was like someone had switched off my brain. The feeling probably only lasted a few seconds, but it felt like forever at the time. Then I caught a glimpse of a Spitfire on my wing, right there with me. It was my flight commander, and he was pointing to his canopy handle. "Bail out!" he was saying.

'That was all I needed. My mind started working again. I opened the canopy, ripped out the radio cables from my helmet, undid my safety harness, turned my ailing plane on her side and clambered out into thin air.'

Gerald was looking up into the sky now. 'I span round and round, getting glimpses of the sea, the sky and the white cliffs of Dover. I didn't know if I was high enough for the parachute to open. All I could do was pull the ripcord and pray.'

'And did it?' Jake said, completely agog.

'Well, I'm sitting here next to you now, aren't I?' Gerald chuckled. 'I floated down very gently, landed in the sea and waited while the Navy sent a gunboat to pick me up. I was home in time for lunch, and back up in the air in a brand new plane the very next morning.'

Jake shook his head. 'Wow. That's amazing.'

'When you experience things like that it makes you realize how precious life is. You've got to try to enjoy every minute. I know I do! Now, I've got some money burning a hole in my pocket, so what say you and I go and visit the gift shop?'

Chapter Seven

The following Monday evening, Jake was sitting at the dining-room table with his head in his hands, once again staring down at the hated Science textbook. The equations and formulas on the page meant nothing to him – they might as well have been written by an alien.

A sick feeling of dread churned in his stomach. This homework was due in tomorrow and if Jake didn't finish it the teacher was bound to make an example of him.

Steve and Mum were in the other room, watching TV. He could ask them for help, he supposed, but that would mean admitting that he'd been lying about how well he was doing at school. Jake could just imagine the disappointed looks on their faces and decided he couldn't bear it.

I need to find my own way out of this mess, he thought. *Got to try harder.*

But try as he might he couldn't make any headway and after countless crossed-out scribblings and wrong answers, he sank into deep dejection. Soon it would be bedtime, then it would be morning and then he'd be at school with nothing to hand in to the teacher …

A knock at the front door jerked him from his mood.

A few moments later, Steve opened the dining-room door. 'Hey, Jake, look who's come to say hello!'

Jake raised his eyebrows in surprise as Gerald appeared, resplendent in a blue pinstripe suit and red waistcoat. He had a battered leather holdall under his arm and a smile on his face.

'Evening, Jake,' he said. 'I've brought some books for you to look at.'

Jake smiled. He was surprised at how much the dapper sight of Gerald had cheered him up. 'Hi, Gerald! I was just finishing my homework.'

Jake saw Gerald's eyes flick to the desperate scribbles on his Science workbook and knew straightaway that he understood how much trouble Jake was in.

'I was on my way back from the dinner and dance at the British Legion and thought I'd pop in to say hello.'

'Would you like a drink, Gerald?' Steve asked.

'Earl Grey would be most welcome.'

As Steve went to make it, Gerald sat at the table and opened his holdall. 'Thought you might like to take a look at these.' He took out some books with photographs of planes on the covers.

'Oh, thanks,' Jake said, flipping through the pages.

Steve returned with Gerald's tea. 'Right, I'll leave you two to talk planes. See you later, squadron leader.'

Gerald turned to Jake with a frown on his face. 'Does he always call you that?'

'Not always, but more often than I'd like,' Jake sighed.

'I can see how you'd find it annoying,' Gerald said with a sympathetic nod. 'But you could do a lot worse than Steve – he's a good man and he means well.'

'I know. He's just so embarrassing sometimes.'

'I actually came round to ask if you fancied another excursion this weekend. I'm off to Duxford on Saturday. They've got a war-bird exhibition on at the museum, so there'll be a whole array of planes and they'll be doing re-enactments and displays. Should be interesting.'

'That sounds great,' Jake said, forgetting his unfinished homework for a moment. 'I'll have to ask my mum but I'm sure she'll say it's OK.'

'Top hole!' Gerald said. 'So, it's Physics homework tonight, eh?' Before Jake could stop him, Gerald picked up the workbook. 'Having trouble?'

Jake resisted the urge to snatch the book back. 'I'm fine,' he said. 'I just need some time to work it out.'

Gerald put on his glasses and peered closely at Jake's work. 'Mmm, well, that's not right ... and neither is that.'

'They're just my initial workings out.' Jake took the book back and slammed it closed.

'Oh, of course,' Gerald said, leaning back in his chair.

'It's always a good idea to get the wrong answers down first and then move on to the right ones.'

'Yeah, course it is,' Jake said. He felt his face burning with shame – for being too slow to do the work that the other kids seemed to know backwards, and for being too proud to ask for help.

Gerald watched Jake carefully as he took a sip of tea. 'I'm pretty good at science, you know – I had to be to join the RAF. Aerodynamics, metallurgy, physics – you name it, I know it.'

Jake looked up, a glimmer of hope growing inside him.

'In fact, some of what you're working on looks pretty familiar to me, as it happens,' Gerald continued. 'You know, it would be quite fun for me to dust off my old skills. Perhaps I could take a proper look at what you're doing?'

Jake gave a nonchalant shrug and opened the textbook. 'If you like.'

'Excellent!' Gerald said, drawing up his chair. 'If we work on it together, we'll get it done in no time.'

And they did. With Gerald's help, Jake not only finished his work, but he learned how to do it himself too. With each correct answer, Jake became more confident. The shame he felt melted away, replaced with a realization that with a little help he could achieve things that before had seemed impossible.

'I enjoyed that,' Gerald said, putting his glasses back into his pocket. 'It's a relief to know my brain is still firing on all cylinders.'

Jake stuffed his books into his school bag, feeling an overwhelming sense of gratitude towards Gerald. 'So you'll pick me up on Saturday?' he asked. 'I'm sure Steve will tag along with us again, and I can ask him or my mum to make us another lunch.'

'Ten o'clock sharp,' Gerald replied. 'And yes to another lunch! The last one was delicious.'

'All right, but this time no eating inside the exhibits.'

Gerald just smiled.

Chapter Eight

The rest of the school week dragged by, with Jake spending lunch and break times on his own, watching the clock inch around to half past three when he could finally escape and go home.

But eventually Saturday came and Jake put all his worries aside; until the creeping dread of school re-emerged on Sunday evening, he was going to enjoy himself.

Gerald arrived in his sports car dead on ten o'clock. Jake and Steve bundled in with three packed lunches and their digital camera. It was another sunny day as they drove down the motorway to the museum at Duxford with the top down and the wind blowing in their faces, chatting about what planes they were most looking forward to seeing.

'You all right in the back there, Steve?' Gerald asked, glancing in the mirror.

'Yeah, I'm fine,' Steve said. 'I'm sure you want to talk planes and I'm happy to listen and learn.'

'You watch,' Jake said to Gerald, 'he'll fall asleep soon.'

'Oh, I nearly forgot to ask,' Gerald said. 'What happened with your homework? Did you hand it in?'

'Yep. I got a "B". The teacher could hardly believe it.'

'He did very well,' Steve said.

'Bravo!' Gerald said. 'But the big question is: could you do the same equations again without any help?'

'I *think* so,' Jake replied. 'I feel a bit more confident about it.'

'Good lad. And remember, I'm always happy to help, but if you're struggling you should tell the teachers. Just be honest – I'm sure they'll understand.'

'I suppose.'

'Not far to Duxford now,' Gerald said, moving into the left-hand lane. 'You can see it over there – look.'

Jake peered out of the window and saw several huge hangars – much larger than the one at Hawkinge – and a long concrete runway. The sun glinted off hundreds of cars in the car park, and there were already crowds of people watching a yellow bi-plane perform aerobatics in the sky.

Jake knew that Duxford had one of the best collections of planes in the country and he could hardly contain his excitement as Gerald found a parking space.

'Here we are,' Gerald said, his eyes shining. 'One of my favourite places in the world – and we have all day to explore.' He looked at Steve and frowned. 'My goodness, he *has* fallen asleep!'

'Told you,' Jake said, and he gave Steve a shake.

After buying their tickets they entered the first enormous hangar. Jake hardly knew where to look first. There were so many amazing planes, some parked on the ground, some suspended from the ceiling and some even he didn't recognize.

As they wandered round discussing each exhibit, Jake's worries about school disappeared from his mind. Steve lagged behind with his eyes fixed on his phone.

There was a Spitfire tucked away in the corner and Gerald stopped and stared at it for quite some time before Jake eventually managed to drag him away to look at the other planes.

'Listen,' Steve said, 'I need to make a few work calls so I'm going to find a quiet spot, all right? Why don't we meet up for lunch in the cafe at two?'

'All right,' Jake said. 'See you there.'

At midday the aerobatics started, so Gerald and Jake went outside to join the crowd and watch the display. Three planes whirled and dived over their heads, engines roaring and the sun flashing in their propellers. Jake was mesmerized, unable to look away as they danced in the sky.

What must it be like to be in control of such a beautiful machine? Jake wondered. *To feel the pitch and roll, the yaw and dive? To be alone and in complete control, to have the freedom to fly anywhere you wanted ... just as Gerald had done during the war.*

Jake turned to ask him about it. Gerald was looking straight up as a silver P51 Mustang fighter flashed overhead, so low they could smell the exhaust. Jake was shocked to see tears streaming down Gerald's face, and his hands, which were normally so steady, were shaking at his sides.

Jake, feeling uncomfortable, looked away, hoping Gerald hadn't seen that he'd noticed. When he looked back Gerald was gone. It was a few moments before Jake saw him hurrying back into the hangar, wiping his eyes with a handkerchief. He had a momentary panic that Gerald was going to drive off without him, but he quickly dismissed the idea – Gerald wouldn't do that.

Nevertheless, Jake knew his friend was upset and he wanted to make sure he was all right, so he squeezed his way through the crowd and followed Gerald into the hangar.

Most people were outside watching the display, so the cavernous space was nearly empty. It was just Jake and the planes – there was no sign of Gerald. Beginning to really worry, Jake jogged around the hangar. He was just rounding the front wheels of a Lancaster bomber when he heard a sort of clumping sound, like something soft knocking against metal.

Jake followed the noise to the far corner of the hangar, where the Spitfire Gerald had stared at was kept. He stopped short when the plane came into view. Gerald was standing on the wing, his face red with effort, tugging at the canopy. Jake could hardly believe it – climbing into an armoured car was one thing, but trying to break into a Spitfire cockpit was something else.

'Gerald!' he hissed, looking around to see if anyone else was nearby. 'What on earth are you doing? Get down from there before we get in trouble.'

Gerald didn't seem to hear. 'Come up here and give me a hand, would you? I can't get the wretched thing open. They must have welded it shut.'

'Probably to keep people like you from trying to get inside.' Jake hurried up to the guard rope. He wished Steve was still with them – he'd be able to make Gerald stop. 'Get down right now. Gerald – this isn't funny. You might hurt yourself.'

'I'll be all right,' Gerald replied with a wave of his hand. 'I'm just going to sit in it for a bit. Seeing those planes out there brought so much back to me, so many memories ... I want to relive those times again, and this might be the last chance I ever get.'

Jake's breath caught in his throat. What did he mean, *the last chance I ever get*?

'Gerald,' he said quietly, 'are you sick? Are you ... dying?'

'Dying? Of course I'm not dying,' Gerald scoffed. 'But I am old and I have to make the most of opportunities like this.'

'No, this isn't right,' Jake said, feeling a flash of anger. 'You can't just break the rules like this, even if you were in the war.' But Gerald didn't reply, and Jake wondered if he'd even heard him.

Gerald clasped both hands over the canopy and braced his legs. 'I'm sure it will open. Just one big pull ... ' His arms shook as he pulled, but the canopy remained stubbornly closed.

'Gerald, don't – '

With a squeal, the canopy slid open, taking Gerald completely by surprise. Losing his balance, he toppled backwards. One hand scrabbled uselessly at the fuselage, but there was nothing to grab hold of.

Gerald gave a cry of pain as he landed hard on his back. The Spitfire's wing was polished smooth and sloped down and to Jake's utter horror Gerald was helpless to stop himself from sliding down and off the trailing edge. He made no sound as his head struck the concrete floor.

For a moment, Jake couldn't move. He just stared at his friend as he lay perfectly still on the ground with his head at a strange angle. Jake's heart thumped against his ribs and there was a high-pitched whine in his ears.

He tried to grasp at the thoughts clamouring in his mind: should he shout for help or call an ambulance? He'd done a first aid course at his last school, but in this most critical moment, when it would actually be useful, he couldn't recall a single detail.

Feeling as if all the strength had drained from his legs, Jake stepped over the guard rope, ran over to Gerald and knelt down by his head. All the life and vitality had disappeared and for a terrible moment Jake thought he might be dead. But then Gerald made a little snoring sound from the back of his throat.

Jake took his hand, feeling the bones under his thin, dry skin. 'Gerald, wake up,' he said, his voice clogging with tears. 'Please, wake *up*!'

'You all right, son? What's happened?'

Jake saw a concerned-looking security guard in a peaked cap standing by the guard rope.

'It's my friend,' Jake replied, his voice wavering. 'He's had a fall ... '

'Right, stay with him and I'll get some help.' The guard turned away and clicked on his walkie-talkie. 'Bev, this is Chris. A gentleman has had a fall in the main hangar. Looks like it could be serious. Can you call an ambulance straightaway, please?'

A voice crackled in reply. 'Will do.'

'I didn't know what to do,' Jake said. 'I tried to stop him, but he ... '

'It's all right. Help's on its way.'

The security guard took his jacket off and placed it over Gerald to keep him warm. When Jake saw the blood around Gerald's head he broke down into helpless sobs.

Chapter Nine

J ake rode with Gerald to the hospital in the ambulance, only leaving his side when the medics wheeled him into a private examination room to be looked at by a doctor.

Jake slumped on to a chair, clasping his hands together to stop them from shaking. He felt numb and confused, as if in some kind of terrible dream. The hospital waiting room was brightly lit and busy, with doctors and nurses seeing to their patients, but Jake didn't notice any of it. All he could think about was the moment Gerald had fallen from the plane and if there was anything he could have done to prevent it.

Dread squirmed in his stomach. What if Gerald *died*? The thought was too awful to consider and Jake felt his eyes fill up with fresh tears.

Gerald had not moved or spoken for the entire journey to the hospital. He'd just lain on the trolley with an oxygen mask on as the paramedic dressed the wound at the back of his head.

'Is he going to be all right?' Jake had asked.

'It's too early to say, I'm afraid,' the paramedic replied. 'But we'll do all we can for him.'

A nurse in a blue uniform came over and knelt down in front of him, interrupting his thoughts. 'Are you Jake Osborne?' he asked. 'Sophie's son?'

Jake nodded.

'I'm a friend of hers. Does she know you're here?'

Jake shook his head.

The nurse put a hand on his shoulder. 'Shall I get her for you?'

It took Jake a few seconds to realize what the nurse was talking about. He'd been so preoccupied he'd forgotten that this was the hospital where his mum worked and she was on shift at that moment. Relief flooded through him like a tidal wave. 'Yes, please,' he said and watched as the nurse hurried off through a set of swing doors.

A few moments later Mum appeared and swept him up in a huge hug. 'Jake, sweetheart, are you all right?'

'It's Gerald. He fell and hit his head. I'm scared he's going to die ... '

'Gerald's with the doctor now, so he's in the best of hands,' Mum said, waiting for Jake to calm down before sitting next to him and taking his hand. 'Tell me what happened.'

Jake told her everything, from the time Gerald seemed to get upset by seeing the air display, to his fall from the Spitfire wing. 'And I can't help thinking it's all my fault,'

Jake finished. 'If I'd have stopped him before he got up there he'd be all right … '

'No,' Mum said firmly. 'This is not your fault, not at *all*. It sounds as if Gerald was being very foolish indeed. You did the right thing by staying with him. I'm very proud of you.' She looked around the room. 'Where's Steve? Was he not with you when this happened?'

Jake shook his head. 'He'd gone off to make some work calls, or something. I tried to phone him before the ambulance came, but there was no signal.'

'So he's still at Duxford?' Mum said with raised eyebrows. 'Right, I'd better get that sorted. He'll be absolutely frantic. I can ask Carol to go and pick him up.' She pulled Jake into a hug. 'Don't worry. It's all going to be fine. Will you be OK by yourself for a bit?'

'Sure, Mum. I'll be fine.'

'Good boy. Be back in a tick.'

* * *

Half an hour later Steve and Carol arrived, looking pale and worried. They didn't see Jake and walked straight past him to the reception desk. After a brief conversation the receptionist pointed to Jake, and Steve and Carol hurried over to him.

'Oh, poor you,' Carol said. 'What an awful thing to have happened.'

'I wish we'd never gone,' Jake said quietly. He looked at Steve. There was an expression on his face that Jake had never seen before: his mouth was tight and his eyes cold.

Jake realized with horror that Steve was *angry*.

'What have the doctors said?' Steve said.

'Nothing,' Jake said with a helpless shrug. 'They took him through there. Mum's with him, I think.'

'I'll go and check,' Steve said. He walked a few paces then stopped and turned back. 'You were supposed to look after him, Jake,' he snapped. 'We trusted you to at least do that.' Then he strode away.

'Steve!' Carol cried. 'That's not fair!'

A sick feeling of guilt welled up inside Jake and he stared down at the floor, wishing he could go back to the beginning of the day and start all over again. There was a whiff of perfume as Carol sat down next to him.

'Don't take any notice of Steve,' she said. 'He didn't mean it. He's just upset and blames himself for having left you on your own with him. We're both very fond of Gerald, you know, and this has been a bit of a shock.'

'I should have stopped him,' Jake sniffed. 'I should have made him get down.'

'Rubbish.' Carol handed him a flowery handkerchief. 'I love Gerald to bits, but he's a stubborn old so-and-so. If he gets it in his mind to do something there's nothing you, me, or *any*body can do to stop him. He's always been like it, as far as I can remember.'

'I just feel so awful about it.'

'Well you mustn't. Gerald speaks very highly of you, you know. He told me last week.'

'Do you think he'll be OK?'

'He got through the war, so I'm sure he can survive a little bump on the head.' Carol smiled, but Jake could tell she was not convinced by her words. 'Oh, here comes the doctor.'

A doctor with long black hair and an immaculate white coat came over with Mum and Steve in tow. Jake couldn't bring himself to meet Steve's eye.

'This is Doctor Khatri,' Mum said. 'She's looking after Gerald for us.'

'Gerald has sustained a nasty bump on the head and he's got some bruising at the base of his spine,' the doctor said. 'We're going to run some tests to see if anything's broken or fractured.'

'Is he still unconscious?' Carol asked.

'No. That's the good news,' Doctor Khatri replied. 'Gerald has woken up and although he's still groggy he is managing to speak coherently. However, I'm going to keep him in for a while so we can take a good look at him. It's always best to be cautious when it comes to head injuries, especially with elderly patients.'

'Can I see him?' Jake asked.

'I don't think he's ready for visitors just yet,' Doctor Khatri replied. 'Perhaps tomorrow.'

'Oh. OK.'

'I'm on shift for a while yet,' Mum said. 'So I'll keep an eye on him.'

'I'm going to stick around too,' Steve said. 'Carol, can you take Jake home and stay with him?'

'Of course.'

Jake's mum kissed him on the forehead. 'I'll be home soon, but I'll call you if there's any news.'

'But I'd like to stay,' Jake said.

'There's nothing you can do. I think it's best you go home and rest for a bit. It's been a horrible day for you.'

'Come on, Jake,' Carol said. 'My car's outside.'

Jake got up and followed miserably after her.

Chapter Ten

When Mum got home that evening she told Jake that Gerald was awake and recovering as well as could be expected. 'You can go and see him tomorrow if you'd like,' she said, much to Jake's relief. So the next day Jake went in with her at the start of her shift.

'He's in here,' she said, ushering Jake into a private room. 'Looks like he's asleep at the moment.'

The room had a large window overlooking the hospital grounds and there was a vase of fresh flowers on the bedside table. Gerald lay propped up on the bed with a bandage around his head. He was snoring.

Mum checked her watch. 'I'd better get back to my ward,' she said. 'Why don't you sit with him for a while? He might wake up soon. I'll pop back later, all right?'

'All right.'

Jake perched on the plastic chair next to Gerald's bed. The sound of the hospital – footsteps, conversations, doors opening and closing – seeped through the walls. The air held a tang of disinfectant.

Gerald was wearing a hospital gown and his hair was less tidy than normal – he looked completely different without his natty suits and ties. Jake was shocked at how much *older* he looked. His skin was paper thin and covered with raised blue veins and his eyes were shadowed and set deep in their sockets.

Jake shuddered as he remembered the sound Gerald's head had made when it hit the concrete. He opened his bag and looked at the model Spitfire he'd brought for Gerald and thought it might actually be a bit tactless to give it to him.

'Ah, hello, Jake. Come to visit me in my new digs, have you?'

Jake looked up and saw Gerald offering him a weak smile. 'Gerald,' Jake said. 'How are you feeling?'

'Oh, right as rain,' he replied, pushing himself up into a sitting position. 'Tickety-boo, in fact. Just having forty winks before lunch.'

'Does your head hurt?'

'Mmm? No! My skull is thick enough to take a little knock.'

But Jake saw Gerald wince and his voice was not as strong as it had been. *He's putting on a brave face,* he thought.

'Do you remember what happened?'

'I remember being jumped by a group of fellows and fighting them off single-handedly, until one of them fetched me a whack over the head with a cucumber.'

He pointed to his bandage. 'Hence this ridiculous get-up.'

Jake felt a surge of relief. It was clear Gerald had not lost his sense of humour. 'No, you climbed on to a plane and then fell off,' he said.

Gerald closed his eyes. 'How awfully embarrassing.'

'Embarrassing? It was frightening,' Jake said, unable to keep the note of anger out of his voice. 'I told you not to go clambering about.'

'I'm a pensioner – I'll do what I like,' Gerald huffed.

'I thought you were dead,' Jake said, feeling his throat tighten. 'And I couldn't stand that, because you're the only friend I have. Promise me you won't do that again.'

Gerald looked at Jake and his stubborn frown softened. 'Oh, very well. I promise not to go climbing on aeroplanes. At least not when you're around,' he whispered.

Jake poked him on the arm. 'Not *ever*, you hear me?'

'Goodness, what a nag you are. OK, yes, I promise. After all, I want to reach one hundred and get my telegram from the Queen.'

Jake frowned. 'What's a telegram?'

'It's a bit like an email but it comes on paper. Now, make yourself useful and get me a drink, would you? A lovely cup of Earl Grey, if you would, with leaves grown in the finest plantations in China and just a *dash* of milk.'

'Er, there's a drinks machine outside, but I don't think they do that ... '

Gerald gave an exaggerated sigh. 'Just water then, I suppose.'

Jake poured some from the jug on the bedside table and handed it to Gerald.

'Boring,' Gerald said. His hand shook as he put the cup to his lips.

Before seeing Gerald again, Jake had decided not to ask him why he had got upset during the display, because he didn't want to embarrass him. But sitting with him now, Jake decided that real friends didn't shy away from asking each other tough questions and he wanted to know what had set Gerald off like that.

He cleared his throat. 'Gerald, before you ran off at Duxford I saw that you were, you know ... upset.'

Gerald gave him a sharp look. 'What do you mean?'

'It looked like you were crying. I wondered if you wanted to talk about it.'

Jake expected Gerald to avoid the question or change the subject. Instead he gazed out of the window, his face creased with sadness. After a few moments he spoke.

'I never expected it to affect me like that. It quite crept up on me. One minute I was enjoying the show and the next I felt this terrible sadness.'

'Why?'

'Seeing that Mustang fly over, I think. The sight and sound of it, the smell of the exhaust. It brought back a lot of memories.' Gerald folded his hands on his lap. 'I had a friend during the war – an American pilot stationed near Biggin Hill who flew Mustangs. Anyway, we hit it off right from the start.'

Gerald turned to Jake, but his eyes were misty and looked far away into the past.

'As the war drew to a close, the Americans were flying their bombers from airbases in England right into the heart of the battle. I'll never forget seeing those monstrous planes taking off. Dozens of them, one after the other. The air would actually *throb* with the noise.'

Jake listened intently to Gerald's quiet voice, realizing he might be the only person Gerald had ever spoken to about this.

'The Mustang was the only fighter with the range to escort the bombers all the way to their targets and that was my mate's job. Every day, like clockwork, up he'd get and fly eight-hour missions.' He shook his head. 'How he did it, I'll never know.'

Gerald paused, deep in thought. Jake waited patiently for him to continue.

'On July 2nd, 1945 he was shot down and killed. The war ended two months later. Rotten luck.'

'I'm sorry,' Jake said quietly.

'I lost a lot of friends back then and I think about them all the time, but his death hit me the most,' Gerald said. 'And after seeing that beautiful Mustang flying over, I had this sudden urge to get into a cockpit. Well, I've certainly paid a high price for my foolishness, haven't I?'

'Well, I think I understand why you did it now.'

Gerald settled back into his pillows. 'You know what I'd really love? To fly over Kent. Feel the freedom of being in a plane and to look down on the land that my friends lost their lives to defend all those years ago. If I could do that I think I could face my end in peace. But I don't suppose I'll get the chance to do that now.' His eyelids drooped, closed, and then he fell asleep.

Jake watched Gerald's chest rise and fall. After careful consideration he took the model Spitfire from his bag and placed it on the bedside table. Then, after lifting the blanket higher over Gerald's shoulders, he left his friend to sleep in peace.

Chapter Eleven

Jake stayed at the hospital until his mum finished her shift. Gerald remained fast asleep, but Doctor Khatri said it was nothing to worry about. 'It just means that Gerald's body is repairing itself,' she'd said, 'and I'm optimistic that he'll make a full recovery.'

This good news made Jake feel much better about the whole thing, but what Gerald had told him about the sadness he felt for his lost friends touched his heart. He was gripped with a desire to do something about it. The question was, what?

Steve and Carol were sitting at the kitchen table when Jake and his mum got home. Jake was still shocked at the way Steve had snapped at him and they had barely spoken since. In fact, Jake felt pretty angry with Steve. Jake felt terrible for what had happened, but he'd come to realize that it was not his fault and Steve had been wrong to blame him.

'Hello, you two,' Mum said, shedding her coat and bag. 'I feel the need for a bath, so I'll leave Jake to tell you how Gerald is.'

There was an awkward silence as they all listened to Mum thumping up the stairs, then Carol gave Steve a pointed look and said, 'I suppose I'll put the kettle on then.'

Jake saw that Steve was looking a bit uncomfortable. *That's better than angry, I suppose,* he thought.

'Come and sit down, Jake,' Steve said, not quite meeting his eye.

'What is it?' Jake asked, aware that Carol was listening to them as she got the mugs from the cupboard.

'Carol's talked some sense into me and made me realize that I owe you a massive apology,' Steve said. 'I blamed you for what happened to Gerald and that was wrong of me. It wasn't your fault, not at all.'

Jake looked down at his hands. 'I tried to stop him, I really did.'

'I know and I feel terrible about what I said. It's just I was shocked and upset and ... I'm very sorry.'

Jake felt all his anger towards Steve drain away. 'I'll forgive you on one condition,' he said.

'What's that?'

'That you stop calling me squadron leader.'

Steve raised his eyebrows in surprise. 'But I thought you liked it.'

'Oh really, Steve!' Carol laughed, coming over with the teas and a plate of biscuits. 'As if anyone wants to be called something as silly as that! So, now that we're all friends again, Jake can tell us how Gerald's doing.'

Jake related what the doctor had said about how Gerald was getting better, but added his own thoughts on how frail he'd looked and how preoccupied he'd been with his past.

'Well, that's understandable,' Carol said. 'A nasty experience like that would make anyone think about things pretty seriously. He tries to hide it, but Gerald's pretty shocked by how close he came to really hurting himself.'

'I'd like to do something for him,' Jake said. 'To cheer him up a bit, get him back to his old self again. I'm just not sure what to do.'

'That sounds like a good idea,' Steve said, looking thoughtful. 'You asked him about his days in the RAF, did you?'

'Oh yes,' Jake replied. 'I ask him questions about it all the time.'

'And he really was a pilot during the war, like we thought he was?'

'Yes. He said he was stationed at Biggin Hill and flew Spitfires.'

'Amazing,' Carol murmured.

'I wonder ... ' Steve opened his laptop.

'What are you looking for?' Jake asked.

'For a way to bring the old Gerald back,' Steve said.

Steve started typing. 'Ah! Here we are! Just what I was looking for.' He spun the laptop round for Jake and Carol to see the screen. The website was called 'Freedom Flights' and there was a picture of a Spitfire below the title.

'"Take a Spitfire for a spin,"' Jake read. '"Fly with one of our qualified pilots and experience the magic of flying this two-seater over the weald of Kent."'

Carol peered over his shoulder. 'This looks amazing! Gerald would love it.'

'But look how much it costs,' Jake said with a frown. 'How could I afford that?'

Steve shrugged his shoulders, but his eyes twinkled with amusement. 'You'll need to use your imagination, Jake,' he said.

'What do you mean?'

'You want to cheer Gerald up,' Steve replied. 'And here's a way you can do just that, but you need the money to pay for it. So ... ?'

Jake thought for a moment. 'I could get a job?'

'I think it would take too long for you to earn enough. And besides, you need to concentrate on your schoolwork. We need to think of something else.'

'Rob a bank?' Jake said with a weak smile.

'Come on, Jake,' Steve said. 'Think! You want to help Gerald, don't you?'

'Of course I do.' Jake frowned, wracking his brains as hard as he could. 'Er, how about some sort of fundraiser event?'

'Now you're on the right track!' Steve grinned.

'Oh, you mean put on a charity event to get one of our brave Battle of Britain pilots back into the air?' Carol said.

'Yes!' Jake replied. 'I'm sure people would jump at the chance to help Gerald when they find out that he was one of the Few.'

'So what sort of event could we lay on?' Steve said.

Jake chewed thoughtfully on a biscuit. 'It's springtime, so how about a garden party? We could make lots of food and drink and have games, prizes and music. People could buy tickets in advance to get in and then spend money when they're there.'

'Oh, this all sounds *marvellous*!' Carol said.

'I'd better make some notes ... ' Steve said, turning back to his laptop. 'We need a name for the event. Something that'll catch people's imaginations and explain exactly what the event is for.' All three of them thought for a while until Steve said, 'OK, let's get back to that later.'

'It's of utmost importance to advertise,' Carol said. 'We need to spread the word far and wide – after all, if no one knows about it, no one will come.'

'We could put up posters,' Jake said. 'Get the local paper to do an article about it?'

'Excellent, excellent … ' Steve said, typing furiously.

'My husband knows people all over the place,' Carol said. 'I'll ask him if he knows anyone at the local radio station. It would be great if they could plug this for us.'

'Local businesses might want to get involved too,' Steve said. 'Food and drink stalls, entertainers … For such a good cause they might donate services to us and it's all free advertising for them, especially if the local paper sends a reporter.'

Jake's frowning face cleared. 'I've thought of a name.'

Steve and Carol looked expectantly at him. 'Hit me, squadron lea – ' Steve stopped himself and clapped his hand over his mouth. 'Oops! Sorry!'

'I was thinking we could call it Hero in the Sky,' Jake said, suddenly nervous that they'd think it was a rubbish idea.

Carol gasped. 'Oh, I *love* it!'

'Hero … in … the … Sky,' Steve typed. 'There. It's official.'

Jake looked out of the window at Steve's garden. 'Will there be enough room out there for this?'

'I don't think so,' Steve said. 'We'll have to hire a venue, I suppose.'

'But that'll cost a fortune,' Carol said. 'No, no, no. We'll host it at *our* place. Bags of room there for stalls and whatnot and it won't cost a penny. Besides, I *love* organizing events. It's what I *do*!'

Overwhelmed, Jake got up and threw his arms around Carol's neck. 'Thank you!'

Carol's look of surprise turned to joy. 'That's all right, dear,' she beamed.

For the next hour they discussed Hero in the Sky in more depth. Mum joined in after her bath and they made a long list of things they'd have to sort out. Jake's head was spinning by the time they finished.

'You'll need to get the school involved,' Mum said. 'If we can get pupils to spread the word and ask their parents to bring them to the event, that'll sell lots of tickets.'

'You could go and talk to the head teacher and ask if the school will really get behind you on this,' Carol said.

'And you can talk to your friends and football buddies. I bet they'd love to come!' Steve said.

Jake's heart sank. What friends? What football buddies? He didn't know *anyone* to talk to at school. He saw that Mum was watching him carefully.

'Oh sure,' he said brightly. 'All my mates will want to come.'

'Great!' Steve said. 'You know, you could do a talk about it during assembly. That would be an amazing way to let people know about this.'

Jake fixed a smile on his face, wondering how his initially brilliant idea had so quickly turned into a nightmare.

Chapter Twelve

The next week was half-term, so Jake could concentrate on organizing Hero in the Sky without having to worry about school. Both Steve and Mum took a few days off work to help and Carol got stuck in with gusto.

At first Jake was a little nervous about leading the organization, but Mum insisted. 'This is your show,' she said. 'Your gift to Gerald, so you're in charge.'

As it turned out, Jake had a real talent for planning. He soon got lost in a whirl of lists, timetables, emails, phone calls and delegating work – even to adults.

They decided to hold the event in two weeks' time. People would pay a small entrance fee, which would go towards paying for Gerald's flight, and enjoy the activities laid on at the party.

Jake wrote an email. In it he described how Gerald had fought in the RAF during the war and how he had lost many friends. He said Gerald had recently suffered a fall and that had sparked a desire in him to take a flight in a plane one last time. Jake then explained how he was putting on a charity event, to raise money for Gerald to fulfil his dream and once again fly in the legendary Spitfire. When the email was finished Jake sent it out to a long list of people and organizations, with a personalized request for their help.

Firstly, Jake needed attractions for the party. So he sent his email to food and drink stall owners. Then he contacted entertainers – jugglers, acrobat troupes, children's entertainers – to see if they would give up an afternoon for a good cause.

Secondly, Jake had to ensure that the event was publicized, so he sent his email to journalists at the local papers and producers at the district radio station, asking if they would mention it to their readers and listeners.

And thirdly, he contacted the local council to ask for any help and support they could offer. 'We need to ensure everything's above board and we obtain all the official permissions and permits necessary,' Steve said.

While waiting nervously to see if they got any responses, the team carried on organizing. There was a lot to do. Jake designed posters and went around the local shops asking if he could put them in their windows.

Carol set about sorting out her house and garden. Mum invited all her doctor and nurse colleagues and Steve used his expertise in social media to spread the word far and wide. Jake started to think that the only person who didn't know what was going on was Gerald, and that was good because he wanted it to be a complete surprise.

Days passed in a whirl and Jake started to worry that no one was going to respond to his emails. But soon replies began to flood in. The local papers and radio station were fully on board, as were the food vendors and local entertainers. They all thought it was a fantastic cause and were fully committed to helping.

Jake was delighted and more than a little relieved. It looked like it was all coming together. But one major worry remained: how was he going to tell people at school about Hero in the Sky when he was totally invisible there?

Chapter Thirteen

Jake knew he had to involve the school because it seemed that the pupils and their parents would make up most of the people at the event. The thought of putting himself forward – the new boy, the boy with no friends – to address the school chilled Jake to his bones, but he knew he had to do it. He had to do it for Gerald.

So he phoned the head teacher on the Friday before school started to ask if he could talk about Gerald and Hero in the Sky in an assembly. The head teacher agreed and the date for Jake to speak was set for Tuesday.

By Sunday he was already dreading it. Standing in front of hundreds of people and delivering a speech from a stage? It was the last thing he wanted to do. But despite his fear, he knew he had to do the best he could. So he used his email as the basis for a short speech and with Steve's help put together a slideshow of photos to accompany it.

After dinner, he went to his bedroom to practise. He'd run through the speech enough times to learn the words by heart when there was a knock on the door.

'Hey, Jake,' Mum said. 'Preparing for the big day?'

'Please don't call it that,' Jake groaned.

'Sorry.' She sat down next to him on the bed. 'I'm so proud of you. I think what you're doing is a-maz-ing. Gerald will be so thrilled. I've spoken to Doctor Khatri and she says he should be going home soon.'

'In time for the event?'

'Yes. When are you going to tell him about it?'

'I don't know. My head's so full of organizing everything I've hardly had time to think about it.' Jake picked up his model Hurricane and twirled the propeller. 'What if no one turns up? What if we only raise ten pence and Gerald is disappointed?'

'Listen,' Mum said seriously. 'I know at least twenty people who are coming and that's just from my ward. Even the patients are talking about it. The radio station is going to start plugging it tomorrow, your posters are up all over town and on Tuesday you're going to speak about it in assembly.'

Jake groaned and flopped back on to the bed. 'I know and I'm *dreading* it.'

'And that's why I'm so proud of you,' Mum said, tickling his stomach. Jake let out a burst of laughter and fell off the bed. 'I know doing stuff like that is hard – no one likes public speaking – but all your friends will be there to support you and I bet they're all going to love your presentation.'

Jake's laughter died in his throat as he sat back down on the bed. He looked at his mum and thought about all the times they'd sat and talked together after Dad had died. It was the worst of times, but they'd been there for each other and promised not to keep secrets.

He looked at her face, at the love in her eyes, and felt an unstoppable urge to tell her the truth about school – and this time he couldn't stop himself. So, in a rush and tumble of words, he confessed his misery: how starting part way through the term had meant he'd missed the chance to make friends; how he spent so much time alone; how far behind he was with his schoolwork.

He told her everything, she listened, and he didn't cry.

'Oh Jake,' she said when he'd finished. 'Why didn't you tell me earlier?'

'I didn't want to spoil everything. You're really happy for the first time in ages ... '

'I'm only happy when you are. And you know what? I'm your mum and I *knew* something was up with you. But I didn't want to force you to talk about it.'

'Well, I have now.'

'Yes, and it's about time.' Mum put her arm around him and pulled him close. 'You're like your father, you know. He would always keep his worries to himself.'

'You think?' Jake said.

Mum nodded. 'I do. So from now on, you *tell* me when something's bothering you and we can deal with it together. All right?'

Jake smiled sheepishly. 'All right.'

'So, solutions,' Mum said in a businesslike tone. 'Your studies are important and we can't have you falling further behind. What subjects are you struggling with most?'

'Maths and Science are the worst. The rest are OK.'

'All right, then, I'll call your teachers tomorrow and we can ask for some extra homework.' Jake opened his mouth to protest but Mum held up her hand. 'No arguments. And besides, it'll only be until you're up to speed.'

'Gerald has helped me before,' Jake said hopefully. 'Could he be my tutor?'

'Nice try,' Mum said. 'But I know you'll end up talking about plancs all evening. Anyway, Gerald needs to concentrate on getting better. No, I'm sure your teachers will be able to help.'

Jake knew that tone and realized there was no point in arguing. And besides, he knew it made sense. 'But what about my other problem?' he said. 'You know, not having any friends.'

'Not having any friends *yet*,' Mum said. 'Look, I know I'm biased, but you are such a fantastic person. If you just put yourself out there a bit people will fall over themselves to get to know you!'

'Well I'll be doing that all right when I do my speech during assembly,' Jake said gloomily. 'Everyone will know who I am after that.'

'You know what I think? After the assembly, and after the Hero in the Sky event, everything's going to be all right for you ... squadron leader!'

Jake smiled and threw a pillow just after his mum ducked out of the door.

Chapter Fourteen

After two fitful nights of sleep, Tuesday arrived. The day of the assembly. Jake peered out of his bedroom window and saw it was a gloriously sunny day.

I hope it's like this on Sunday, he thought.

He ran over his speech in his mind as he put on his school uniform, then went downstairs to a breakfast he had no appetite for. Mum and Steve were already waiting for him in the kitchen.

'Hey, champ,' Mum said. 'All set?'

'I guess so,' Jake said, feeling a resurgence of butterflies in his stomach. 'I'll be glad when it's over.'

Steve pointed to the clock on the wall. 'In two hours it will be,' he said. 'Before you even know it.'

'Steve's taken the morning off to take you into school,' Mum said, pouring out some cereal for Jake.

'I can help you set up your presentation,' Steve said, 'and cheer you on from the side of the stage.'

'Really?' Jake said, feeling grateful and relieved. 'Are you sure?'

'Sure as sure,' Steve grinned. 'Always good to have a friendly face nearby when you're undertaking a challenge.'

'I've got to go.' Mum gave Jake a kiss. 'I'll be thinking of you!'

'Bye, Mum.'

Jake forced himself to eat some cereal and then, after ensuring he had everything he needed for the assembly, he and Steve drove to school half an hour earlier than usual. After Steve signed in as a visitor, they went straight to the school hall.

The hall was big enough for the whole school to fit inside and brightly lit by floor-to-ceiling windows. There was a stage at one end and an enormous projector screen. The head teacher had told Jake to set everything up for his talk and then he would introduce him when everyone had arrived. The assembly was due to start at nine, just under thirty minutes away.

'I'd get up there now if I were you,' Steve said. 'Get a feel for it.' He went to the side of the stage and started loading Jake's presentation on to the computer. 'Here we go … just get this sorted and you're all set.'

But Jake wasn't listening. He was looking at the vast expanse of floor and imagined it filling up with children and teachers, all waiting to hear him speak. His legs felt weak, his mouth dry and a great weight had dropped into his stomach. His heart started to pound and before he knew it he was gasping for air.

'I can't … I can't … do this,' he gabbled.

Steve was by his side in an instant. 'It's all right,' he said, gently taking his shoulders. 'Just look at me, OK? Remember, you've practised this over and over, so you're totally prepared.'

'But … I … can't … do … it … in … front … of … the … whole … school … ' Jake said, taking a gasp between every word.

'Yes, you can.' Steve's voice was calm and he was smiling encouragingly. 'You've got this, buddy.'

'I … I … *can't*!'

Steve turned him round so he was facing the projector screen where a picture of Gerald looked down at him.

'Yes you can,' Steve said. 'And you will, because you're doing this for your friend up there. And I promise you, when you're done with this speech, you'll be so proud of yourself. In fact, you'll feel like you can do *anything*. So, keep breathing.'

'I … *am* … breathing!'

'Good. Now, just slow it down a bit … That's right … slow it down … '

Jake felt his breath begin to slacken and slow. After a minute or so it had returned to normal. His nerves still jangled, but he felt better. He looked at the clock. Quarter to nine.

It will all be over in half an hour, he thought. *Just keep that in your mind.*

'Better now?' Steve asked.

Jake nodded and managed a little smile.

They both looked up when they heard the door open and a stream of pupils began to file in behind their teachers.

'Remember, I'm right here with you,' Steve said, leading Jake to the side of the stage.

Jake watched with a sick feeling of dread as the hall filled up with row upon row of whispering children. A few cast curious glances in his direction. He began to run the lines over in his head and was pleased to find that he remembered them word for word. Perhaps this would all be OK after all.

The head teacher came in last and marched on to the stage, looking confident and in control. *That's how I need to look,* Jake thought. *If I look like that no one will know how nervous I am.*

'Are you ready?' the head teacher asked him.

Jake nodded. 'I'm ready.'

'Excellent! I'm totally behind what you're doing, Jake. I think it's wonderful and I know the rest of the school will too.'

'Thank you,' Jake said, feeling a trickle of confidence seep into him.

'So,' the head teacher said, 'I'm going to give you a quick introduction and you can take it from there.'

And he was off, striding to the middle of the stage and gesturing for quiet. The hall fell silent.

'Good morning, everyone,' he said.

'Good morning, Mr Banks,' the school replied.

'We're doing something a little different today. Someone else is going to talk to you – a fellow pupil who only joined our school a few months ago. I know you will all listen to him just as you would to me or any of your teachers.' He turned to Jake and held up his arm. 'So, big round of applause, please, for Jake Osborne.'

This is it, this is it, this is it, Jake thought wildly.

He only began to move when Steve gave him a gentle push. Putting one foot in front of the other, Jake walked, head down and clutching his speech in both hands, until he reached the middle of the stage. The clapping slowly died away and – apart from a few coughs – silence fell.

Jake turned to face the audience. A sea of expectant faces looked up at him. He felt as if a huge spotlight was being trained on him and the whole world was watching. From the corner of his eye he saw Steve, his face illuminated by the computer screen.

He's probably feeling more nervous than I am, Jake thought. *If I can just get started I think I'll be OK.*

He licked his lips as he tried to recall the first line of his speech. There was a second of panic before it came to him.

'Hello, everyone.' Jake pointed to the projector screen behind him. 'I'd like to talk to you about my friend Gerald ... '

Chapter Fifteen

Jake's speech went really well. He didn't trip up over his words and he spoke calmly and loudly, ensuring that his voice carried to the furthest reaches of the hall. The terrible nervousness that had eaten away at him vanished the moment he opened his mouth.

By the time he'd finished and answered some questions about the event from some of the teachers and pupils, he felt a wave of relief. But more than that he felt proud of himself. He'd done it! He'd overcome his fear and done it. *Go me!* he thought as he strode off the stage towards a beaming Steve, the sound of applause ringing in his ears.

Jake hardly had time to stop for the rest of that week. Every spare moment he had – in the evening and during lunch and school breaks – he looked over his 'to do' lists, checking and replying to emails, and racking his brains for yet more things that needed to happen to make the event a success.

When he came home on Friday evening he found Mum, Steve and Carol at the kitchen table. 'Hey, everyone,' he said. 'What's the news?'

'All good,' Steve said. 'We've heard back from the Council and they're happy for the event to go ahead as planned. And get this! The Mayor of Canterbury has heard about this and he's asked if he can come and open the event. What do you think of that?'

Jake gasped. 'You mean the guy who wears the big chain and robe?'

'The very same.'

'That's amazing!' He felt a flutter of nerves. 'This is turning into a really big deal ... '

'It is and it's all down to you,' Mum said, sliding a plate of biscuits over to him.

'And I've been busy as a bee too,' Carol said. 'The house and garden are ready and they look an absolute *picture*. The pavilions and bunting are up, and I've strung lots of outdoor lights around so it will look really *magical* when the sun goes down!'

'And you know what else?' Mum said. 'So far this event hasn't cost a penny to put on. Which means that all the money we make can go towards Gerald's flight.'

'That's because everyone is so behind what you're doing,' Carol said. 'Everyone's mucking in from the goodness of their hearts. It's really rather moving, isn't it?'

'That reminds me, treasurer,' Steve said, taking a large brown envelope from his pocket and giving it to Carol. 'Here's the money for the tickets from my colleagues at work.'

'Marvellous!' Carol said. 'I can add that to what we've already made.'

'So,' Jake said, hardly daring to answer the question. 'How much *have* we made?'

The three adults exchanged a quick glance. 'Well,' Mum said, 'not enough to pay for the flight.'

'But,' Steve quickly added, 'lots of people will just turn up and buy a ticket on the gate. That's where most of the money will come from.'

'I hope so,' Jake said. 'Otherwise this whole thing will be a complete disaster. What if the Mayor turns up and there's only us there?'

'Don't be silly!' Mum said. 'Honestly, everyone knows about it and everyone wants to come.'

'OK then,' Jake said, managing a smile. 'How is Gerald doing?'

'More good news,' Mum said. 'He's pretty much recovered and back to his old self. He's at home now and so far he hasn't got a clue what we're up to.'

'We thought it would be nice for you to go and tell him tomorrow,' Steve added. 'How does that grab you?'

'Cool,' Jake said. 'There's something else I want to do for him.' He opened his bag and took out a picture frame that he'd bought on the way home. 'I'm going to try and find a photo of Gerald from when he was a pilot and put it in here.'

'What a lovely idea,' Carol said, 'But where are you going to find one at such short notice?'

'There's masses of photos online,' Jake said, 'and I've learned how to search for really specific ones using key words.'

Jake's mum kissed the top of his head. 'You go off and do that while Steve and I cook dinner. You'll stay, won't you, Carol?'

'Oh, don't mind if I do!' Carol said.

* * *

Jake went to his room and turned on his computer. As it booted up he turned his mind towards the coming event. Despite Mum, Steve and Carol's reassurances, he was worried it would be a total disaster.

What if none of the entertainers bothered to show up? What if they didn't sell any tickets on the gate? What if the food stalls sold bad burgers and everyone got sick? What if it rained?

'Stop fretting,' he murmured to himself. 'You've done all you can. Now we just have to wait and see.'

He began his image search and soon became lost in the seemingly endless photographs of pilots, planes and airfields. Most were in black and white, but some were in colour.

It would be so cool if I could find a colour photo of Gerald in his Spit, Jake thought, imagining his friend's face when he presented it to him in the frame. He scrolled through the reams of RAF pilot images, reading the captions and hoping to see Gerald's name. After an hour Jake's eyes were hurting and Gerald still hadn't shown up. There was a chance, he realized, that no such photo existed.

But, refusing to give up, Jake changed the search word 'pilot' to 'airbase personnel', hoping that might throw up some new images. Cupping his chin in his hand, he began to scroll down the page.

Mum's voice floated up from the bottom of the stairs. 'Hey, Jake! Dinner's nearly ready!'

'Be right there,' he replied.

He was about to go downstairs when a black and white photo at the bottom of the screen caught his eye. It was of two young men standing in front of a Spitfire. In the background Jake could see a large hangar and a row of military-looking trucks.

Jake's heart leapt. The man standing on the left looked a *lot* like Gerald. He was the right height and had the same swept-back hair, although it was much darker in the photo. However, it was the twinkling eyes and mischievous smile that convinced Jake that this was indeed his friend.

And yet there was something strange about the photograph. The other man wore a flight suit, helmet, goggles and fur-lined leather jacket, so was clearly a pilot. But Gerald was wearing oil-stained overalls and had a tool belt strapped around his waist.

Frowning, Jake clicked through to the website where the photo came from and read the caption underneath.

Flight Sergeant William J. Blazkowicz stands in front of his Spitfire. Alongside him is Corporal Gerald Speke, one of his mechanics.

Jake read the caption again, not quite believing it. He scrolled down the page and saw other photos of Gerald in his overalls, always referred to as a mechanic. Jake shook his head, trying to make sense of what he was seeing.

Gerald had not been a pilot during the war. He'd never flown Spitfires.

The man who Jake had thought was his friend had *lied* to him.

Chapter Sixteen

J ake stared at the photos. He felt numb and confused. The closeness that he'd felt for Gerald shattered as he realized that he didn't really know him at all. If he'd lied about being a pilot, what else had he been dishonest about?

He remembered the story Gerald had told him about his disastrous patrol over the English Channel and how he missed flying so much. All lies. Jake turned the monitor off, not wanting to see the photos any more.

Then, through the feeling of betrayal and confusion, another realization hit him like a blow to the head. His Hero in the Sky event, which was all set to happen on Sunday, had been organized on the principle that a veteran RAF pilot was going to be given a chance to fly in a Spitfire again.

It was Jake who had swallowed Gerald's lie and it was Jake who had then repeated it to everyone else: Mum, Steve, Carol, all the people who had generously agreed to help with the event and all the people who had spent their money on tickets.

And all the kids at school who had listened to him speaking in assembly!

Jake put his head in his hands as a sick feeling of panic

rose up from his stomach. What were they all going to say when they found out the truth?

Jake felt a cold fury build inside. He'd tried to do something nice for his friend, but instead Gerald had made a fool of him. He'd be the laughing stock at school, and it was all Gerald's fault.

He went downstairs, picked up the phone, returned to his room and dialled Gerald's house. As it rang he felt his heart pounding in his chest. Despite his fury, Jake was mindful that Gerald had only just returned from hospital and it would be wrong to upset him with an argument.

Don't shout. Stay calm, he thought. *Just ask him why he lied.*

There was a click as the phone was picked up on the other end. 'Hello, this is Gerald Speke speaking.'

At any other time Jake would have laughed at that, but not today. Forcing himself to keep his voice calm, he said, 'You weren't really a pilot, were you?'

'Jake? Is that you?'

'Yes, it's me. And I said that you weren't really a pilot, were you.' Jake was finding it hard to keep the anger from his voice.

'Jake, are you all right? You sound upset.'

'I *am* upset!' Jake snapped. 'I thought you were my friend and you *lied* to me.'

'But ... I ... '

'I looked online for photos of you during the war and I found out that you were an RAF mechanic.'

Jake let the words hang. There was a long silence on the other end of the phone, broken only by Gerald's breathing.

'Well?' Jake said. 'Have you got anything to say?'

He'd half expected Gerald to deny his accusation, for him to say that Jake had made a mistake. Instead Gerald sighed and said, 'Yes, you're right. I wasn't a pilot, I was a mechanic.'

Hearing Gerald admit his deception broke Jake's control and the anger he had so far held down erupted. 'How could you have lied to me like that? You told me stories about things that never happened, and I *believed* you! Do you realize how that makes me feel?'

'I never meant for you to feel – ' There was a pause. 'Hang on a minute, why were you looking for photos of me on the Internet?'

'I wanted to find a picture of you as a pilot and get it framed. It was going to be a present.'

'Oh, Jake, I'm sorry. Let me come over and explain—'

'No!' Jake nearly shouted. 'Don't come round. I don't want to see you. I don't *ever* want to see you again!'

He hung up and threw the phone on the bed.

When he looked up he saw his mum standing in the bedroom doorway with a tea towel in her hand.

'Jake,' she said. 'What on earth is going on?'

Chapter Seventeen

Mum, Steve and Carol stared at Jake, their faces utterly bewildered.

'I don't understand what you're saying,' Steve said. 'You told us he was a pilot in the Battle of Britain.'

Jake's anger had receded, but he didn't yet regret shouting at Gerald down the phone. He flipped Steve's laptop open on the kitchen table and searched for the page where he'd found the photos. 'There,' he said. 'That's Gerald and he's a mechanic. It says so in the caption and he admitted it on the phone.'

'But why would he lie like that?' Mum said, sitting down heavily in a chair.

'He was always a joker,' Carol said, 'but I never thought he'd go this far. How long would he have kept up the deceit if you hadn't found out, I wonder?'

'It's a horrible thing to do,' Mum said. 'Upsetting Jake like this … '

'Of course we're going to have to consider what to do about the event,' Carol said. 'People are contributing their time and money to put an ex-pilot back into the sky. What are they going to say when they find out that's not actually the case?'

Mum put her head in her hands. 'Oh goodness, all my friends. And the *Mayor* of Canterbury's coming! What are we going to do?'

'Did you tell Gerald about the event, Jake?' Steve asked.

Jake shook his head. He still felt shaky as the adrenalin from the phone call began to sour in his veins. 'I should have checked his story long before organizing all this,' he said. 'This is my fault.'

'Oh nonsense, dear,' Carol said, patting his hand. 'Steve and I have known him far longer and we didn't have a clue about his past, so why should you have known any better? We were *all* taken in.'

'And who could have predicted that he'd have said something so dishonest?' Steve added.

'Well, the event's on Sunday, so we need to decide what to do right now,' Mum said.

Before they could turn their minds to the problem there was a knock on the door. Jake answered it and found an elderly lady on the doorstep wearing a smart skirt and blouse, polished leather shoes and a hat pinned jauntily to the side of her thick grey hair.

'Er, hello,' Jake said. 'Can I help you?'

'I hope so,' she replied. 'Are you Jake Osborne?'

'Yes, I'm Jake.'

'The same Jake Osborne who's organizing the Hero in the Sky event on Sunday?'

Jake's face dropped. *What now?* he wondered.

'That's me,' he said.

'Oh good,' the lady said. 'My name's Maggie and I'd like to talk to you about Gerald. It's important.'

Jake raised his eyebrows and stepped aside. 'Come in,' he said, leading her through to the kitchen. 'Maggie, this is my mum, Sophie, her partner Steve and his sister Carol. We're all organizing the event. Everyone, this is Maggie. She says she wants to talk to us about Gerald.'

They looked surprised, but Mum got up and offered Maggie a cup of tea and a seat at the table.

'Thank you,' Maggie said, sitting down and carefully unpinning her hat. 'I'm sorry to barge in like this. You're probably wondering who I am and what I'm doing here.'

'Well, I'm certainly intrigued,' Carol said. 'Are you a friend of Gerald's?'

'We were friends,' Maggie said. 'But we've not spoken since he moved to Germany years ago. So you can imagine my surprise when I saw him being talked about on the local news yesterday. It brought a lot of memories back for me, I can tell you.'

She smiled wistfully for a moment then carried on. 'Anyway, after seeing your event reported on the news I felt I had to come and speak to you personally.'

Jake, Steve, Carol and Mum exchanged glances and leaned closer to Maggie. 'Go on,' Steve said.

'I think what you're doing is marvellous,' Maggie said, looking a little uncomfortable. 'But you're under an unfortunate misapprehension. You see, Gerald was never a pilot. He was in the RAF, but he was a mechanic.'

Steve gave a bark of laughter. 'You're ten minutes too late, Maggie,' he said. 'We just found that out.'

'Oh, I see,' she replied.

'How do you know that he wasn't a pilot?' Jake asked.

'Ah, well, you see I knew him very well back in the war,' she said. 'I was in the RAF at Biggin Hill too.'

Jake's ears pricked up. 'Really? Did you work in the operations room?'

'No, dear. I was a pilot.'

There was a stunned silence that Maggie seemed to rather enjoy.

'But ... you're a woman,' Jake blurted out.

Maggie laughed. 'Well spotted! But I assure you, I was a pilot during the war.'

'Wait a minute,' Steve said. 'I've read about this. What was it now? The Air Transport something?'

'Top marks,' Maggie smiled. 'I was one of about two hundred female pilots in the Air Transport

Auxiliary. We flew air ambulances and brand new planes from the factories to the airbases.'

Jake was astonished, not just by the fact that he was talking to a real pilot, but that he'd never heard of the Air Transport Auxiliary.

'What planes did you fly?' he asked.

'Oh, you name it, dear, and I've flown it. Spitfires and Hurricanes, of course. But also Barracudas, Lancasters, Oxfords, Battles. The list goes on, but my favourite was the de Havilland Mosquito. Beautiful planes and *fast*!'

Jake and the others stared in awe at this well-spoken woman sitting at the kitchen table drinking tea.

'Was it dangerous?' Carol asked.

'Flying a plane is always dangerous, dear,' Maggie said. 'And we were at war. The enemy could pounce at any time. And remember, we weren't combat pilots so the planes we flew didn't even have any ammunition. We couldn't fight back. Quite a few of my friends lost their lives, I'm afraid.'

She put her cup down. 'Anyway, I didn't come here to rabbit on about myself. I'm here because of Gerald. Does he know about the event you're organizing?'

Jake shook his head. 'No. It was supposed to be a surprise for him.'

'But it was him who gave us the surprise by turning out to not be a pilot,' Mum said angrily.

'Well, in his defence, I'm sure he would have come clean if he'd known what you were organizing for him,' Maggie said.

'Did you know him well?' Jake asked.

'Well enough to know not to take everything he says too seriously,' Maggie said with a smile. 'The funny thing is, when we met back in 1940, he also told me he was a pilot.'

Jake raised his eyebrows. 'He did? Why?'

'He was pretty sweet on me,' Maggie said. 'I think he thought it would impress me enough to agree to go out with him, but I saw right through it!'

'So he was a liar back then as well,' Jake said bitterly.

'Now listen,' Maggie said. 'I know you're upset and you've every right to be. But Gerald is a good person and although he wasn't a pilot he did his duty and for that he deserves your respect.'

Maggie paused and then said, 'And I'll tell you something else you don't know about Gerald – he saved my life. If it wasn't for him I wouldn't be here today. And neither would my children and grandchildren. As far as I'm concerned, he is a hero.'

Chapter Eighteen

'Really?' Steve said. 'What happened?'

'Well,' Maggie said, 'it was August 1940 and I was transporting a brand new Spitfire from the factory at Castle Bromwich to Biggin Hill. I was about a mile away when I got a warning over the radio that there was an enemy bombing raid in progress.'

'What did you do?' Jake asked.

'I had to think fast. I was only a few minutes away – I could actually see the runway – and knew that there might be enemy fighters about. I was flying low, had no airspeed and was in no position to escape if they saw me. So I decided the best thing to do was to land and get to shelter.'

Maggie paused, seemingly lost in the past. Agog, Jake, Mum, Steve and Carol waited for her to continue.

'I was young and had only been flying solo for a few weeks, so when I saw the black specks of the bombers approaching the airfield at low level from the other direction, I thought my heart would stop. But I'd made up my mind and I continued my approach. As I got closer I saw people scurrying about and the flicker of the anti-aircraft guns.

'I felt the bump as I touched down – I thought I was home free. But then there was a huge flash and a bang, and a great plume of mud and concrete and smoke flew into the air from the other end of the runway. Then another explosion, and another, each one getting closer.'

'How terrifying,' Carol murmured.

'I couldn't take off again because the runway was ruined. All I could do was throttle back the engine and use the rudder to try to steer my Spit away from the explosions. I veered off the concrete and on to the grass, still going at about eighty miles an hour. I was only just in time. Another bomb hit right next to me.' Maggie shook her head. 'The noise was deafening. Then the shockwave flipped the plane up into the air. The port wing sheared off and suddenly I was upside down.

'The canopy cracked, but luckily didn't break as the plane slid for what seemed like ages. I felt clods of mud and concrete thundering down on to the metal. I remember thinking that I was going to be buried alive. Then the plane stopped. I heard more explosions and the wail of the sirens.'

Maggie took a sip of tea.

'It was dark. Smoke was all around me. I was hanging upside down, so dazed I couldn't even undo my seatbelt.

I felt blood running down my face and under my flight helmet. Then I saw orange and knew that the plane was on fire. I tried to move my arms ... pain like I'd never experienced hit me like a train. I cried out then. Anyone would. Both my shoulders had been dislocated.'

Jake winced and involuntarily rubbed his hands over his shoulders.

'I thought that was it,' Maggie said. 'I thought I was about to die. Then, through the pain and the noise I heard a sound, a heavy *thunk*, right by my left ear. Suddenly I was covered in a shower of acrylic and a blast of air. A man's hands reached into the hole and undid my seatbelt. I remember that they were covered in grime and oil.

'Next thing I know I'm free from the seat and being dragged out through the hole. If I thought the pain was bad before, I was wrong. I screamed and screamed, but my rescuer took no notice. The fire was getting worse, I could feel it against my face. And who knew how long it would be before it touched some spilled fuel and exploded?

'My rescuer got my top half out, then grabbed me under the arms and *heaved*. I popped out like a cork from a bottle and he threw me over his shoulder and ran towards the shelters. I remember my arms dangling by my sides, unable to move. And the clamour: sirens, screams, smoke. It was terrible. That's when I fainted. The pain, you see.'

'What happened when you woke up?' Steve asked.

Maggie smiled sadly. 'The raid was over and I found myself in the infirmary along with all the other wounded. I was lucky. Thirty-nine people were killed that day.'

'And the man who rescued you was ... ?' Jake said.

'Gerald. You must understand, the plane could have exploded at any second, but he didn't give up until he'd got me out.'

'He's a real hero,' Steve murmured.

'He is,' Maggie said.

Jake thought hard about what he had just learned and felt his anger towards Gerald melt away. 'I'd like to go and see him,' he said quietly. 'I need to say sorry for shouting at him.'

'You can go tomorrow,' Mum said.

'I'll come with you if you don't mind,' Maggie said. 'I'd like to see the old fellow again.'

'We still have a bit of a problem with the event though,' Steve said. 'It's been advertised as a fundraiser to put a Spitfire pilot back in the air, but we know now that that's not true. So what are we going to do?'

'It would be such a shame to cancel,' Maggie said.

'Wait a minute,' Jake said. 'You were a pilot, Maggie! We could have the fundraiser for you. Would you like to fly again?'

'Oh no, dear,' Maggie said. 'I wouldn't want that, although thank you for the offer. But I do have an idea that might solve your problem.'

'We're all ears,' Carol said.

'How about you just tweak the event a bit?' Maggie said. 'Instead of raising the money for Gerald, raise the money for a charity instead. I'm sure everyone in the town would get behind a good cause like that.'

Mum looked at Jake. 'It's your event, love. What do you think?'

'Please say yes,' Carol said. 'You've put so much work into it. And the garden looks such a picture.'

Jake grinned. 'A charity fundraiser it is,' he said. 'Thanks, Maggie!'

Chapter Nineteen

As agreed, Maggie arrived at Jake's house early the next morning. Together they walked to Gerald's house on the other side of town, leaving Mum, Steve and Carol to organize the last bits and pieces for the rebranded charity event.

Jake was nervous about seeing Gerald again, but he couldn't resist asking Maggie questions about her time as a pilot. She was happy to answer and didn't seem to mind reminiscing about the past.

'I look back on that time and despite the fear and danger I remember many good times too. Gerald was a big part of that,' she said as they stopped outside his house. 'I'm really looking forward to seeing him again after all these years.'

They knocked and after a few moments Gerald opened the door. He opened his mouth to speak, but when he saw Maggie no words followed.

'M ... Mags?' he said at last.

'Hello, Gerald,' she said with a smile. 'How are you?'

Gerald took a step forward. 'I don't believe it! Maggie! You ... you look just the same.'

Maggie gave a shriek of laughter. 'Liar!'

'But what are you doing here?'

'I'll tell you after you've put the kettle on,' she replied.

Gerald turned a sheepish gaze to Jake. 'Hello, Jake. How goes it?'

'It's all right, Gerald,' Jake said. 'I'm not going to shout at you. I've come round to say I forgive you and to ask if we can be friends again.'

'Oh, well, that would be marvellous,' Gerald beamed.

'On one condition,' Jake said. 'No more lies. I want to know the *real* Gerald, not a made-up one.'

'Deal,' Gerald said.

'How are you, by the way?' Jake asked. 'All better?'

'Fighting fit!' Gerald twinkled. 'Now, tea for three is it?'

* * *

Jake didn't say much as they drank tea and ate biscuits; he was happy to listen to Gerald and Maggie laugh, reminisce and catch up after many years apart. They got on so well it seemed as if they'd been best friends for years.

Gerald turned to Jake as Maggie got up to put the kettle on again. 'I'm very sorry I didn't tell you the truth, Jake,' he said. 'I know you say you've forgiven me, but I feel I should try to explain.'

'OK,' Jake replied.

'It started off so harmlessly,' Gerald said. 'You presumed I'd been a pilot, so I just went along with it. But the longer it went on the harder I found it to admit the truth.'

Maggie tutted as she turned on the kettle.

'The thing is, I desperately wanted to be a pilot, so I hot-footed it down to the RAF recruitment centre as soon as I was old enough.' Gerald looked down at the table. 'But I failed the medical exam. My eyesight wasn't up to scratch so there was no chance of me flying. I was devastated. What I wanted more than anything had been taken from me and there was nothing I could do about it. They offered me training to become a mechanic, so I agreed. I would have done anything to be close to those beautiful planes.'

'It was an important job,' Jake said. 'Without you the planes wouldn't have been refuelled, rearmed and repaired to continue the fight.'

'And,' Maggie said, sitting back down, 'if you'd been in a plane taking part in a mission somewhere instead of being on the ground during the raid, I wouldn't be here today.'

'Well,' Gerald said, 'that certainly makes the disappointment worthwhile.'

'Too right it does!' Maggie said. 'Now then, Jake, I think it's about time you told Gerald about the exciting event that's happening tomorrow.'

Chapter Twenty

To Jake's astonished relief, the charity event was a huge success. Everything, including the bright and sunny weather, was perfect.

The stallholders had set up in Carol's garden the night before the event and the entertainers had arrived early in the morning. By the time the Mayor opened the gates at ten o'clock there were already a hundred people eagerly waiting outside.

The growing crowd wandered around the beautiful garden, happily chatting, picnicking and watching the jugglers, tumblers and puppet show. The Mayor did a speech using a borrowed karaoke machine, encouraging everyone to spend lots of money.

Gerald and Maggie strolled together, arm in arm, answering questions from people who had seen Gerald on the television. People were amazed when they found out that Maggie had been a pilot and she was interviewed by a journalist from a national paper.

Jake was standing under an oak tree watching a local band when three kids he recognized from his class wandered up to him. He remembered that they were called Jamie, Lance and Francine.

'Hey, Jake,' Lance said. 'This event's pretty good. Did you really organize it yourself?'

Jake said, 'Er, well, I had some help ... '

'Yeah, it's all right, actually,' Francine said, surveying the scene.

'So,' Lance said, 'is this your house?'

Jake was somewhat taken aback that they were talking to him as if they were already friends, but he took it as a good sign. 'No – it's my mum's partner's sister and her husband's house,' he said.

'Uh huh,' Lance said. 'Complex.'

'Anyway, thought we'd say hi.' Jamie waved his hand.

Feeling less and less shy by the moment, Jake smiled and said, 'Hi.'

Francine was looking at him with her head cocked. 'So, how come you don't talk to anyone at school?'

Jake stared at her, not knowing what to say. He shuffled his feet. 'I don't know,' he muttered. 'It's just I don't really know anyone, I suppose.'

Jamie, Lance and Francine exchanged a glance.

'You should have just come and said hello,' Jamie said.

'We don't bite,' Lance added.

'Anyway, hang out with us now if you want,' Francine said, already heading towards the lake at the bottom of the garden. 'Race you!'

'Sounds good!' Jake said, following them and feeling relief wash over him like summer sun.

* * *

After a fun and frantic afternoon, Jake's new friends had to go home, so Jake went off in search of Carol. He found her by the ice cream van.

'Good timing as usual,' she said, handing him an ice cream.

'Ooh, thanks!'

'Well, I don't know about you, but I deem this a monumental success.'

The sun was beginning to dip below the trees, but the evening was warm and there were still lots of people milling about.

Jake nodded, feeling simultaneously happy and exhausted. 'I think so too,' he said. 'I wonder how much money we've made?'

'Oh, hundreds if not thousands, I should think,' Carol said. 'It will make a big difference to a lot of people.'

Jake saw a smiling Gerald and Maggie wander past, then he looked up and saw a plane leaving a bright white chalk line across the sky. 'It's a shame though,' he murmured.

'What is?' Carol asked.

'That Gerald won't get to achieve his dream. You know, to actually fly a Spitfire.'

'Yes, it *does* seem a shame, doesn't it?' Carol said.

Jake saw a familiar gleam in her eye. He smiled, nonplussed. 'What are you looking so pleased about?'

Carol took Jake's arm, her face breaking into a beam. 'I've been talking to some of my clients who are here today,' she said. 'They've been really inspired by all your hard work putting this event together. They work with some generous donors who would love to help make a hero's dream come true ... '

Chapter Twenty-One

Two weeks later, Jake, Mum, Steve, Carol, Maggie, Francine, Jamie, Lance and Gerald arrived at Biggin Hill airfield. It was a gloriously sunny Saturday. Perfect weather for Gerald's flight in a Spitfire.

Everyone was armed with cameras and feeling very excited. Gerald had been unusually quiet on the journey, but he hadn't stopped smiling once.

They were greeted by the pilot who was going to fly Gerald in the two-seater Spitfire.

'Well, Gerald,' he said, 'it's my pleasure to take you for a spin. It'll be for about an hour so we can go quite far and I'll be happy to give you control of the plane for a while, if you'd like.'

Gerald was still smiling. 'That would be marvellous.'

'I'm so jealous,' Francine said as the pilot took Gerald away to get kitted out in flying gear. 'I'd love to go for a flight, too.'

'Better start saving your pocket money then,' Lance laughed.

Five minutes later Gerald and the pilot made their way towards the runway. Gerald, decked out in a leather jacket and flying helmet, beckoned Jake over.

'I'd like you to see the plane close up,' he said, 'and hear that big-cat roar.'

As they rounded a wooden hut they saw the Spitfire sitting on the end of the runway. Jake was struck anew by its beauty. With its narrow, almost delicate fuselage, its bright red nose pointing towards the sky and its wide and rounded wings, it looked like the perfect flying machine.

Gerald slowed down and stopped. He wiped something from his eye.

The pilot turned to him. 'Are you feeling all right, Gerald?' he asked.

'Oh yes,' Gerald replied. 'It's just being back at Biggin Hill and seeing that beautiful plane waiting there ... it brings back a lot of memories. Happy, sad, but all precious.' He smiled at Jake. 'Thank you for this. I can't tell you how much ... '

Jake gave him a gentle push towards the pilot. 'Don't mention it.'

The pilot turned to Jake. 'I heard what you did to raise all that money. So, if you'd like, I'll take you up for a spin later on. What do you say?'

Jake couldn't say anything. He just stood there with his mouth open as the pilot helped Gerald into the cockpit.

Gerald laughed as the pilot clambered aboard and started the engine. 'Of course he'd like to! He's going to be a flyer when he grows up.' He saluted then slid his visor down. 'A flight in a Spitfire. At last, after all these years … '

The pilot spoke a few words to Gerald and then slid the canopy closed. Gerald gave Jake a thumbs up and then put his oxygen mask on.

Jake's ears rang as the pilot opened the throttle. The Spitfire crept forward. Blue fumes snorted from the exhausts. Sunlight flashed on the whirling propellers.

And then, with a roar that split the air, the legendary plane swept down the runway and leaped into the sky like a lion.

Airborne. Free. Skyward bound.

All About the
Air Transport Auxiliary

Jake thought that he knew almost everything about World War Two, so he's amazed to find out from Maggie about the female pilots who worked for the Air Transport Auxiliary (ATA). Though these women did brave and important work during the war, not many people have heard of them.

The ATA was formed at the start of the war to make use of experienced pilots who were not able to take part in active combat. Instead of going abroad to fight, they transported aircraft to military airfields around the UK.

To begin with, only male pilots were included. However, as the demands on the ATA grew, it soon became obvious that it would need more pilots to keep running. So in 1940, despite strong opposition from some men, the first female recruits joined the ATA. They became known as the 'Attagirls'.

The first Attagirls

The first eight female recruits were accepted on 1st January 1940. All eight women had learned to fly before the war and were experienced and competent pilots, but they carried a great weight of responsibility on their shoulders. Their involvement had to be a success if more female pilots were to be recruited. Their first flights were difficult, taking place in harsh winter conditions. But the female pilots' efficient and impeccable service persuaded those in power to recruit more women, and soon there were many more female pilots from all over the world: America, Australia, Canada, Poland and many other countries. Maggie is a fictional character, but if she'd existed she would have been one of 168 female pilots in total.

Life as an Attagirl

At first the female pilots were only given small, single-engine Tiger Moth planes to fly, but soon they were flying 38 different types of aircraft. Their job of transporting new planes from factories to the airfield meant they had to be able to fly every kind of plane.

The female pilots were never directly involved in combat and so they carried no ammunition – but this didn't stop the enemy planes attacking them. It was a very dangerous undertaking; 15 female pilots were killed during their time in the ATA. These women risked their lives, knowing their contribution was helping the war effort.

Equality in the air

As the Attagirls began to take on more and more flying duties, they started campaigning for equal pay.

Despite facing the same dangers and the same long hours of flying, the female pilots were earning 20% less than their male counterparts. In the summer of 1943, they were finally successful and the women were paid the same as the male pilots.

After the war

The female pilots of the ATA made an immense contribution to the war effort, but they knew their days as professional pilots were numbered. By the end of the war, there were so many trained male pilots that opportunities for women were limited again.

Many of the Attagirls, however, had a passion and enthusiasm for flying and so continued to do so, while others became involved in gliding or teaching – but it wasn't until 1992 that women were allowed to fly jet aircraft in the Royal Air Force. In 2009 another milestone was reached when the first female pilot was appointed to the Red Arrows.

As well as being an invaluable part of the war effort, the 'First Eight' women who flew for the ATA in 1940 led the way into the skies for military female pilots.